DISABILITY DISCRIMINATION

Bullet Points

*keeping it short
and to the bullet point!*

DISABILITY DISCRIMINATION
© Robin Hawker: March 2020
All rights reserved

email: robin@worklaw.co.uk
website: www.worklaw.co.uk
telephone: 07549 168 675

Imprint: Independently published
ISBN: 9798629108535

updated and republished: May 2023

- LaTeX typesetting
- and cover design
- by Quaystone Books
- www.thrillers.pub

Disclaimer

Bullet Point Booklets on UK employment law are written from the point of view of an employer but should be of interest to employees who need to check that they are being treated fairly and in accordance with the law.

This series is entitled *UK employment law*. But this is not an accurate title as the UK does not have a single system of law. The focus in this booklet is on the law of England and Wales which is the same for both countries. Employment laws in Scotland and Northern Ireland are broadly the same as in England and Wales but may differ occasionally.

Employment law is complex and changes frequently due to political, social and economic pressures, and the law might have changed by the time you read this booklet: the publication date is on the title page.

Please view this booklet as a brief guide to employment law. It is not a complete guide. The author makes every reasonable effort to ensure that the information given and the opinions expressed in this booklet are a reasonably accurate summary of the relevant law at the time of publication, but this booklet is intended for guidance only and is not intended to constitute and should not be used as a substitute for legal advice on any specific matter. No liability for the accuracy of the content of this booklet, or the consequences of relying on it, is assumed by the author or the publisher.

Contents
Disclaimer
Other Bullet Point Booklets
About Worklaw

The Equality Act 2010

When we refer to *the Act* we mean the *Equality Act 2010* which governs discrimination, including disability discrimination.

The Equality and Human Rights Commission

The Equality & Human Rights Commission (the Commission) promotes equality and good practices in relation to equality, including in the workplace.

The Commission has powers to issue codes of practice and conduct investigations into compliance with the Act, including compliance in the workplace, and may support individuals to bring a claim of discrimination when appropriate; support includes financial support.

Definition of a disability

Under the Act a person is disabled if they have:

> a physical or mental impairment which has a substantial and long-term adverse effect on their ability to carry out normal day-to-day activities.

Impairment may be a physical or mental or both.

Substantial (a bad heart) means something more than minor (a bout of flu).

Long-term means that the impairment has lasted or is likely to last for at least a year.

Normal day-to-day activities are not defined by the Act, but are likely to include:

- lifting a shopping bag;
- driving a vehicle;
- using a computer;
- plus any activity which could reasonably be called *normal day-to-day*.

The following are medical conditions that are likely to come within the above definition of an impairment (the list is not exhaustive):

- diabetes;
- arthritis;
- depression;
- schizophrenia;
- phobias;
- personality disorders;
- autism;
- dyslexia;

- learning disabilities;
- asthma; and
- heart disease.

More than one seemingly minor impairment, if combined, might amount to a disability.

Point to note: it is *day-to-day* activity, not activity in the workplace, which is the legal test.

Exceptions to the standard definition

Persons who have certain medical conditions are deemed *automatically* to have a disability for the purposes of the Act.

For example:

- cancer;
- multiple sclerosis;
- blindness.

Progressive medical conditions

By a progressive condition we mean a medical condition which increase in severity over time; for example, motor neurone disease.

Where a person has a progressive condition initially the effect on their ability to carry out normal day-to-day activities may not be sufficiently serious to amount to *a substantial adverse effect*.

Nevertheless, they are treated as disabled if their condition is likely to have *a substantial adverse effect* on their day-to-day activities *in the future*.

This means that a person with a progressive condition may qualify for protection as a disabled person before the adverse effects of their condition become serious.

Excluded medical conditions

Examples of medical conditions which are not deemed in themselves to be a disability under the Act include:

- alcoholism;
- kleptomania;
- hay fever.

However, an excluded medical conditions could develop into an included condition.

For example, if alcoholism caused cirrhosis of the liver, the cirrhosis could be an impairment.

Extended definition of *employee*

The Act protects both job applicants and those in employment and extends the definition of employee to include (the list is not exhaustive):

- workers;
- agency staff; and
- some self-employed persons (if classed as a worker).

Definition of a worker

The simple definition is:

> a person is generally classed as a worker (instead of being an employee or being self-employed) if they have a contract to do work or provide services personally, and only have a limited right to subcontract the work.

However, in practice, many factors must be taken into account when deciding whether the person should be classed as a worker.
Our Bullet Point Booklet called *Employment Contracts* explains what factors are relevant.

Past disability

The Act protects persons who are no longer disabled, but who had a disability in the past.
For example, it would be disability discrimination not to give an applicant a job because they still suffer debilitating effects resulting from treatment for the past impairment.

Reasonable adjustments

An employer must make *reasonable adjustments* to assist a disabled employee or job applicant.
For example, a reasonable adjustment for an employee who is colour-blind might include utilising computer software which does not rely upon the operator being able to distinguish colours.
An alleged failure by an employer to make a reasonable adjustment is a frequent cause of complaint to an employment tribunal.
We discuss the obligation on employers to make reasonable adjustments for disabled employees in the section headed *Failure to make reasonable adjustments*.

Whether there is a disability

As stated in the above definition of a disability:

- an impairment may be a physical or mental, or both;
- it must be long-term (at least a year);
- and have a substantial adverse effect on the person's ability to carry out normal day-to-day activities.

In many cases, unless the medical evidence is clear, an employer will dispute that an employee is disabled.

Where there is a doubt, the onus is on the employee to show that they come within the definition of disabled for employment law purposes.

Whether an impairment is a disability will depend on all the facts and circumstances of the individual case.

It may be disputed that the impairment has lasted at least a year or is likely to last a year.

And it may be disputed that that the impairment has a substantial adverse effect on day-to-day activities.

Sometimes, the parties produce conflicting medical evidence and opinions and it is then up to an employment tribunal to decide.

Normally, when a claim is one of disability discrimination, the tribunal panel comprises an employment judge sitting with 2 lay members (an employer and an employee).

Disfigurement

To decide whether a disfigurement or deformity is a disability for the purposes of employment law it is necessary to consider factors such as:

- is it permanent?
- how noticeable is it?

If the disfigurement is severe it is very likely to be classed as a disability.

Obesity

Obesity is not in itself a disability but the effect of obesity could amount to a disability if, for example, the obesity resulted in the restricted movement of limbs.

Employer's knowledge of the disability

Unless the employer knew, or should have known, that the person was disabled, an employer cannot be liable for:

- *direct* disability discrimination;
- discrimination arising from disability;
- or failure to make reasonable adjustments;

An employer will not be liable for *harassment* unless the employer knows, rather than perceives, that the person discriminated against was disabled.

However, an employer can be liable for *indirect* discrimination even though they are unaware of the disability.

Vicarious liability

Under the doctrine of *vicarious liability* an employer can be held responsible for a discriminatory act by an employee, done in the course of their employment, even though the employer did not cause or authorise the act. This doctrine applies to employment law generally and not just to disability discrimination.

Both the employer and the discriminating employee could face claims in an employment tribunal of disability discrimination, and both could be ordered to pay compensation to the disabled person who was discriminated against.

The employer will be held to vicariously liable unless they can show that they had taken all reasonable steps to prevent employees, in the course of their employment, discriminating against a disabled person.

At the very least, to stand any chance of defending a claim of vicarious liability, an employer should have a written policy against discrimination in a staff handbook or in a stand-alone policy document.

Complaints of discrimination

A complaint of discrimination should be handled in accordance with the employer's *grievance policy* or procedure, which usually means, handled informally or formally, depending on the complainant's wish, the seriousness of the complaint and the possible action required to address the complaint.

If an employer becomes aware of discriminatory behaviour, in the absence of a complaint, it is incumbent on the employer to take immediate action to stop the discriminatory behaviour.

Informal procedure

Using an informal approach, unless clearly the wish of the disabled employee, can be a risk, as the employer might be accused of not taking a complaint seriously enough.

An employer must explain to every one concerned that, although being dealt with informally, the complaint is still being taken seriously.

If the complaint is particularly serious then it should be dealt with in accordance with a formal grievance procedure.

An employer should remember that even if they think that they are acting in the best interests of a disabled person, they may still be deemed by an employment tribunal to have discriminated against that person, possibly under the doctrine of vicarious liability, referred to above.

Formal procedure

As advised in the previous section, an employer should have a written policy in regard to discrimination of any sort, and its prevention.

Except for very minor complaints, which can be dealt with informally, perhaps by a line manager having a quiet word with the employee who caused the minor complaint, a complaint of disability discrimination should be dealt with formally in accordance with the procedure set out in the written policy.

Types of disability discrimination

The Act lists 6 types of disability discrimination:

- (A) direct discrimination;
- (B) indirect discrimination;
- (C) harassment;
- (D) victimisation.

The 4 types of discrimination above are also relevant to other types of discrimination, such as sex or race.

There are 2 more types which apply solely to disability discrimination:

- (E) discrimination arising from a disability;
- (F) failure to make reasonable adjustments.

(A) Direct discrimination

Direct discrimination can be sub-divided into 3 types:

- *ordinary* direct discrimination;
- direct discrimination *by association*;
- direct discrimination *by perception*.

Examples

An example of *ordinary direct discrimination* would be a decision not to employ a person who has cancer when they would have been offered the job but for the cancer.

An example of *direct discrimination by association* would be a decision to dismiss an employee because occasionally they have to take time off work to care for (are associated with) a close relative who is disabled.

An example of *direct discrimination by perception* could be an employee who is shunned by colleagues at work because they think (perceive) that she might be autistic (a possible disability).

The essential question to ask is - why did the disabled person receive less favourable treatment than others?

Comparators

A person claiming *direct disability discrimination* must show that they have been treated less favourably when compared to a real or hypothetical comparator whose circumstances are not materially different to theirs.

The comparator may be non-disabled or have a different disability to that of the disabled person.

The emphasis is on *circumstances*: the circumstances must be similar to (shared) by the employee claiming direct disability discrimination and by the comparator.

The shared circumstances must be those which the employer took into account in deciding to treat the disabled employee as it did, excepting the disability, but comparing the claimant's abilities to those of the comparator.

The disabled person and the comparator must have abilities that are materially the same.

There will be no direct discrimination if the comparator has the same abilities (or inabilities) as the disabled person, and would have been treated the same way by the employer.

(B) Indirect discrimination

An employer is potentially liable for *indirect discrimination* even though they are unaware of the disability, and even though they do not intend to discriminate.

Indirect discrimination is when the employer (or prospective employer) puts in place *a provision, criterion or practice* (PCP) which applies equally to a group of employees (or job applicants) but has, or will have, the effect of putting a person or persons with a certain protected characteristic (a disability) at a particular disadvantage when compared to others in the group, and the employer is unable to justify the PCP (see the next section).

The relevant protected characteristic is the disability.

An employee or job applicant claiming indirect discrimination must show how they have been personally disadvantaged, as well as how the discrimination has or would disadvantage other employees or job candidates with the same protected characteristic (also disabled).

Provision, criterion or practice (PCP)

The Act does not define a *PCP*.

A PCP is likely to include any rule or procedure in an employment contract or a staff handbook or a stand-alone policy document, or in any other relevant document.

However, a PCP does not have to be in writing and could arise from, say, *custom and practice over time*.

A relevant PCP might include, for example:

- how staff are recruited;
- what benefits are given to staff;
- how candidates for redundancy are chosen.

Employers should monitor carefully their policies and practices for inadvertent discrimination.

Policies and practices which were not discriminatory when they were first introduced may become discriminatory over time, perhaps because of a change in the composition of the workforce.

Comparators

A claim of *indirect discrimination* requires a comparator (see *Direct discrimination* above).

Any comparative disadvantage that would be suffered by those of the claimant's particular disability as a result of the PCP (see previous section) must be measured against actual or hypothetical persons whose circumstances are not materially different.

Objective justification

In some limited circumstances, *indirect discrimination* may be objectively justified if the employer can prove it is a proportionate means of achieving a legitimate aim.

For an employment tribunal to agree that there was a proportionate means of achieving a legitimate aim an employer must show:

- a good business reason; and
- that the employer's actions were proportionate, appropriate and necessary.

To succeed in showing in showing objective justification both of the above bullet-points would need to apply.

Basically, it is not easy for an employer to persuade an employment tribunal that indirect discrimination was justified.

Health and safety

Sometimes employers will suggest, relying on objective justification (see section above), that health and safety is the legitimate aim. But employers should ensure that any action taken in relation to health and safety is proportionate to the risk to health and/or safety.

Any risk assessment should take account of:

- a disabled person's circumstances;
- reasonable adjustments to mitigate risk;
- the obligations not to discriminate; and where appropriate,
- the disabled person's own views.

In general, there must be a balance between protecting against the risk to health and safety and restricting disabled people from access to employment.

Disabled people are entitled to make the same choices and to take the same risks within the same limits as non-disabled people.

Health and safety law does not require employers to remove all conceivable risk, but to ensure that risk is properly appreciated, understood and managed.

(C) Harassment

Harassment is much easier to define than indirect discrimination.

The conduct must have the purpose or effect of violating a person's dignity or creating an intimidating, hostile, degrading, humiliating or offensive environment for that person.

Basically, it is words or conduct, unwanted by the person, which is related to a person's disability.

Conduct amounting to harassment related to a disability could include the obvious:

- nicknames;
- insults.

And could also include less obvious conduct related to the disability such as:

- inappropriate questions;
- unwanted jokes;
- ignoring the person.

When jokes or comments are unwanted it is usually no defence to say that the words used were intended as banter.

In deciding whether the conduct complained of amounts to harassment, each of the following must be taken into account:

- the perception of the person making the complaint of harassment;
- whether it is reasonable for the conduct to have the effect which is complained about;
- any other relevant circumstances.

As with direct discrimination, harassment may be based on the disability of a third party or on disability generally.

Making a joke about a disability in the presence of a disabled person even though that person is not, directly, the subject of the joke, could be deemed to be harassment.

(D) Victimisation

Victimisation occurs when an employee suffers *a detriment* because, in good faith, they:

- made an allegation of discrimination; and/or
- supported a complaint of discrimination; and/or
- gave evidence about discrimination; and/or
- raised a grievance about discrimination; and/or
- did anything else covered by the Act.

A *detriment* is defined as something that causes damage, harm, or loss, for example, being overlooked for promotion.

Victimisation could occur if the employer merely suspects the employee of doing one or more of the things listed above and then treats the employee as a troublemaker to their detriment because of this suspicion.

(E) Discrimination arising from disability

The concept of *discrimination arising from disability* was introduced in 2010 by the Act. Discrimination under this heading occurs when:

- an employer treats a disabled person unfavourably because of something arising in consequence of their disability; and
- the employer cannot show that the treatment is a proportionate means of achieving a legitimate aim.

Unfavourably means that the disabled person has suffered a disadvantage. A disabled person, claiming this type of discrimination, does not have to compare their treatment with how someone else is treated (a comparator). It is only necessary to demonstrate that the unfavourable treatment is because of *something arising in consequence of the disability*, such as:

- an inability to work unaided;
- a need for regular rest breaks or toilet breaks;
- slower typing speeds;
- regular hospital appointments;
- difficulties in using public transport;
- a need for specialist computer equipment;
- a need for private and/or quiet working environment.

The person does not need to refer to a provision, criterion or practice (PCP) (see section above) or show that persons sharing their particular disability are placed at a group disadvantage.

Unacceptable words

Some particular words and phrases regarding disability are clearly unacceptable.

Other words, inoffensive in themselves, can cause unintended offence, when used in the context of a disability.

The general advice is to avoid words or phrases that imply negativity. For example, the words *suffering from* may infer that the employee's disability has a *negative impact* on the employee.

Another example is to avoid referring to employees without a disability as *able-bodied*, as this suggests they are better able to do their job whether or not this is the case.

Possibly, *non-disabled* is a better word to use when there is a need to say who is disabled and who is not.

Confidentiality

Normally, an employee's disability should be kept confidential by the employer unless the employee gives clear permission for the information to be shared.

Occupational requirement

In certain circumstances, it may be lawful for an employer to specify that applicants for a job must have a particular protected characteristic under the Act; in other words, a particular disability. This is known as an occupational requirement.

However, it is not enough for an employer to decide that they would prefer to employ someone who has a particular disability, unless the disability in question is crucial to the job, and is *a proportionate means of achieving a legitimate aim.*

Basically, it will be rare for an occupational requirement to be justified.

Positive action

An employer can use positive action to encourage disabled persons to apply for a job.

However, an employer does not have to select disabled applicants over non-disabled applicants, just because they have a disability.

The employer is entitled to select the best candidate solely on merit.

The Employment Appeal Tribunal

The Employment Appeal Tribunal (EAT) has summarised the proper approach to claims for discrimination arising from disability as follows:

- The employment tribunal must identify whether the disabled claimant was treated unfavourably and by whom.
- The employment tribunal then has to determine what caused that treatment, focusing on the reason in the mind of the alleged discriminator, and it might be necessary to determine the conscious or unconscious thought processes of that person, but keeping in

mind that the motive of the alleged discriminator in acting as he or she did is irrelevant.

- The tribunal must then ask whether the reason for the treatment complained of was something arising because of the disabled claimant's disability. This is an objective question and does not depend on the thought processes of the alleged discriminator. That reason might arise from, or be linked to, various causes.
- The knowledge required is of the disability; not knowledge that the something leading to the unfavourable treatment was a consequence of the disability.

Points to note

- When the claim is one of discrimination arising from disability a defence of objective justification might be available (see the section above headed *Objective justification*).
- An employer cannot be liable for discrimination arising from disability unless they knew (or should have known) about the claimant's disability. But an employer must do all they can reasonably be expected to do to find out if a worker has a disability.
- A disabled person, claiming this type of discrimination, does not have to compare their treatment with how someone else is treated (a comparator). It is only necessary to demonstrate that the unfavourable treatment is because of something arising in consequence of the disability.
- And a disabled person does not need to refer to a provision, criterion or practice (PCP) (see section above) or show that persons sharing their particular disability are placed at a group disadvantage.

(F) Failure to make reasonable adjustments

Allegations that an employer has discriminated against a disabled person by failing to make a *reasonable adjustment(s)* to take account of the disability, is a frequent claim in a claim of disability discrimination in an employment tribunal.

A *reasonable adjustment* is defined as *a change or adaptation to the working environment that has the effect of removing or minimising the impact of the individual's impairment in the workplace so they are able to undertake their job duties, or apply for a job, without being at a disadvantage.*

More favourable treatment

An employer can lawfully treat employees and job applicants who are disabled more favourably than non-disabled employees or applicants through making reasonable adjustments.

Specifically, employees or applicants who are not disabled are prevented from claiming discrimination on the grounds they have been treated less favourably because of the reasonable adjustments made for a disabled colleague/applicant.

Factors to consider in employment

The 3 main factors an employer should consider in assessing what reasonable adjustments might need to be made for a disabled employee are:

- change how things are done?
- physically change the workplace?
- provide extra equipment or get someone to assist the disabled employee?

Examples of a reasonable adjustment

Examples of a reasonable adjustment for a disabled employee could be:

- allowing the employee to work flexible hours;
- providing a suitable office chair for someone with a bad back;
- allowing an employee with Crohn's disease to work as close as possible to a lavatory;
- providing written instructions in large type for an employee with poor eyesight.

Recruitment

- An employer can only ask health-related questions in very limited circumstances before making a job offer.
- In particular, questions about previous sickness absence are classed as questions that relate to health or disability and must not be asked.
- However, an employer should ask whether a job applicant needs any reasonable adjustments, often called *access requirements*, for any part *of the recruitment process*. Asking this question is not considered to be the same as asking a job applicant if they are disabled, although the applicant might volunteer this information in answer to this question. If possible, the employer should then make the required adjustment.

- A prospective employer should ask a job applicant whether they need any reasonable adjustment if it is apparent that they have a disability, even though the disability has not been mentioned.
- An obligation to make a reasonable adjustment may arise once the employer could be expected to know that the job applicant has a disability. Only after offering the job, should an employer ask the successful applicant what adjustments they will need to do the job.

Factors in assessing what is reasonable

Whether a proposed adjustment is reasonable usually depends on an assessment of a number of factors, including:

- is the proposed adjustment practical?
- will the adjustment be effective in overcoming or reducing the disabled employee's disadvantage in the workplace?
- does the employer have the resources to pay for the adjustment?
- will the adjustment have an adverse impact on the health and safety of others?

Flexible working

Employees have a statutory right to request flexible working once they have worked continuously for the same employer for 26 weeks.

Flexible working is also something that an employer might need to consider as being a reasonable adjustment in regard to a disabled employee irrespective of whether the disabled employee has been employed for 26 weeks.

While, generally, an employer can turn down requests for flexible working on certain *business grounds*, the employer could not refuse a request for flexible working by a disabled employee if the request amounted to a reasonable adjustment.

Knowledge of the disability

The employer does not have a legal duty to consider and make reasonable adjustments if the employer does not know about the employee's disability. However, the Equality and Human Rights Commission's *Employment Statutory Code of Practice* says an employer is expected to do all it can reasonably to find out if an employee is disabled.

Points to note

- An employer has a legal duty to make reasonable adjustments.
- It is the employer who must bear the cost of the adjustment.

- Adjustments can often be simple and inexpensive.
- It is good practice for employers to seek medical advice before making a decision on a proposed adjustment.
- The focus must be on the employee's ability to function on a day-to-day basis rather than on a medical diagnosis.
- It is the employer who makes the final decision whether to make an adjustment.
- Adjustments only have to be reasonable; an employer is not required to change the basic nature of a job.

Reasonable adjustments

It is usually said that there are 7 areas in employment when reasonable adjustments are most likely to be necessary. These areas are:

- recruitment;
- employment terms;
- sickness absence;
- promotion opportunities;
- training opportunities;
- dismissal;
- redundancy.

Probably, *recruitment* is the stage which has the most potential for causing an employer to breach the law against disability discrimination. A job-applicant can make a claim of disability discrimination because they are not offered the job; they do not have to be an employee to make a claim.

Recruitment

When recruiting, an employer must not:

- reject a disabled applicant because it would need to make reasonable adjustments if they employed that disabled person;
- include wording in a job advertisement which would discourage disabled applicants;
- include in a job advertisement any reference to mental and physical health or fitness which might relate to a disability unless such a reference is necessary because of the nature of the job.

With regard to the last bullet point, an example of a necessary reference to physical fitness might be, that a scaffolder working at heights should not suffer from bouts of giddiness.

An employer can refuse to make requested adjustment if that adjustment would change the core nature of the job.

Each case must be judged on its own specific circumstances, which means that two seemingly similar cases may have different outcomes; one requested adjustment might be adjudged to be reasonable whereas the requested similar adjustment might be deemed to be unreasonable. If in doubt, an employer is advised to assume that the requested adjustment is reasonable unless the employer can give very persuasive reasons as to why the requested adjustment is not practical or is otherwise not reasonable.

Job application forms

Job application form could be discriminatory, unintentionally. For example, to insist on the form being *filled out in your own handwriting* may inadvertently discriminate against those whose disability may affect their ability to write.

Employers should examine their job application forms, when still in draft, to ensure that only necessary questions are asked which are relevant to the job on offer. For example, to ask if the applicant has a driving licence, when the job on offer does not entail driving, would be discriminatory in regard to someone who does not hold a driving licence by reason of a disability.

Job interviews

Interviewers should not ask questions of the applicant, which are not relevant to the job.

This is general advice and not advice which is specific to disability discrimination.

To ask an applicant if they jog might be asked in the context of *small talk* but could be perceived as potential discrimination against someone with difficulty in walking.

Questions about health

Under the Act, it is generally unlawful for an employer to ask questions about a job applicant's health, absences from work or disability before offering them employment.

The Act is intended to stop disabled job applicants being *screened out* early in a recruitment process.

The Act applies to any person recruiting people for work. In most cases, this will be an employer or someone working on their behalf such as a recruitment agency.

It is also unlawful for an employer's representative to ask a job applicant questions about their health or disability. This means that an employer cannot refer an applicant to an occupational health practitioner or ask an applicant to fill in a questionnaire provided by an occupational health practitioner before a job offer is made.

As stated previously, and important to remember: questions about previous sickness absence are classed as questions that relate to health or disability and must not be asked.

However, there are few specific circumstances when questions about health and disability can be asked during the initial stages of a recruitment process. These circumstances are set out in the next paragraph.

Allowed health questions

There are certain specific situations in which health or disability questions are allowed to be asked during the early stages of the recruitment process, as follows.

- To establish whether the applicant can take part in an assessment to determine their suitability for the job.
- To determine whether any reasonable adjustments need to be made to enable a disabled person to participate in an assessment during the recruitment process.
- To find out whether a job applicant would be able to undertake a function that is intrinsic to the job. An *intrinsic function* of a job is a function which, if it could not be performed, would mean that the job could not be carried out.
- To monitor diversity among job applicants. Monitoring information should be kept separate from application forms in order to minimise the risk that this information will influence the selection process.
- To support positive action in employment for disabled people. The Act allows an employer to take positive action to assist people who are disadvantaged or under-represented in employment.
- If there is an occupational requirement for the person to be disabled.

Making an offer

Once the employer has decided that a job applicant meets their requirements, the employer might make the applicant a job offer, or place the applicant in a pool of successful applicants to be offered jobs as vacancies arise. At this point, the employer is allowed to make the job offer conditional upon the successful applicant meeting the employer's health or other requirements. The Act does not then prevent the employer asking questions relating to health or disability. The employer may, for example, need to ask questions to determine whether a successful applicant would be eligible for job-related benefits, or would need reasonable adjustments to enable them to do the job.

If an employer rejects an applicant solely because the person has a disability, this is direct discrimination and is unlawful.

At whatever stage of the recruitment process an employer gains information about a person's disability, the employer must not use that information to discriminate against the disabled person because of the person's disability.

Employers can make job offers conditional upon satisfactory responses to disability questionnaires or satisfactory health checks. However, they must ensure that they do not discriminate against a disabled job applicant on the basis of any information gained from such questions or health checks.

Potential claims

If a disabled person thinks that an employer has acted unlawfully by asking questions about health or disability that are not permitted, that person can complain to the Equality and Human Rights Commission, which has powers to take enforcement action against the employer.

A person does not need to have a disability to complain to the Equality and Human Rights Commission in this situation.

A person cannot bring an Employment Tribunal claim against an employer for asking unlawful questions about disability and health. It is only where such questions are asked and the employer uses the information gained to discriminate against the person that he or she can bring a disability discrimination case in an Employment Tribunal. If an employer asks unlawful questions but does not use the information to discriminate against the person because of disability (for example the disabled person is nevertheless offered the job) no discrimination has occurred and there is no case to bring.

Employment terms

By employment terms we include pay and the other terms and conditions which should be included in an employment contract.

It is important for employers to ensure that there are no terms and conditions in their employment contracts which disadvantage or exclude people because of their disability, perceived disability, association with someone with a disability, or something linked to their disability.

Sick pay

An employee absent because of disability-related sickness must be paid no less than their contractual sick pay, if the employer provides it in the terms of employment. But an employer does not have to automatically extend contractual sick pay beyond the usual entitlement.

If an employer does not offer contractual sick pay, an employee should usually be paid statutory sick pay if eligible.

If the reason for the extended absence is because of the employer's delay in implementing a reasonable adjustment so the employee can return to work, maintaining full pay is likely to be a further reasonable adjustment.

Sickness absence

Employers should be careful that their *sick pay* policy does not discriminate (intentionally or unintentionally) against employees who have the benefit of the Act otherwise they risk claims in an employment tribunal.

In particular, an employer should be careful how it treats an employee who is absent from work for a medical reason which could amount to a disability within the definition of the Act.

Medical reports

Sometimes employers suspect that an employee is not ill but is absent for non-medical reasons, and threaten to take disciplinary action.

However, bearing in mind that it does not take much for an Employment Tribunal to find that a medical condition amounts to a disability, it is usually wise for employers to give the employee the benefit of the doubt, unless they have reason to believe, backed up by evidence, that the employee is not actually ill or is staying away from work for a reason other than their medical condition.

If the absences go beyond a reasonable time then, at that point, the employer should ask the employee to agree to the employer obtaining a medical report with a prognosis as to when the employee is likely to be able to return to work. Usually, it is the employer who has to pay for the report which may be expensive depending on the complexity of the alleged medical condition.

A medical report might also be necessary to clarify whether there are reasonable adjustments which should be made if the employee does have a disability.

Sickness procedure

By law (*s.1 Employment Rights Act 1996*) and employer must give an employee a document (*a written statement*) setting out certain mandatory information which includes terms in their sick pay policy regarding an employee absent for a medical reason.

It is advisable to consider and make reasonable adjustments to the wording of the policy so that disabled employees are not at a disadvantage because their disability prevents then from complying with the policy. An example, might be a requirement *to inform the employer by 8 am that the employee will not be at work and that a failure to inform by this time would be a disciplinary matter*. Such a strict requirement might be discriminatory against an employee whose disabling medical condition prevents them from communicating during a bout of the condition.

Absence *triggers*

Employers need to be careful about *absence triggers*, by which we mean the number of days' absence when managers consider warnings, and possibly dismissal, unless attendance at work improves.

Employer should ensure that a trigger is reasonable for all employees including disabled employees and those employees who might be disabled. If necessary, an employer should lengthen the trigger to a reasonable extent thereby making a reasonable adjustment.

Employers should remember that disputes over sickness absence linked to disability might be considered under another type of discrimination claim; that is, *discrimination arising from disability*, and that a discrimination claim under this heading does not require the disabled employee to compare their treatment with that of another employee.

Potentially reasonable adjustments

Examples of potentially reasonable adjustment could be:

- allowing disabled employees time off work for medical treatment;
- recording disability-related sickness absence separately from other illness absence;
- phased return to work after disability-related absences;
- working from home when practical;
- moving to another job role more suitable for someone with the disability in question.

Assessing reasonable adjustments

Assessing whether a proposed adjustment would be reasonable should includes taking into account not only the impact on the employee, but also on others in their team regarding workload and resources. A *reasonable adjustment* should include:

- agreeing reasonable attendance levels;
- removing uncertainty about taking disability-related time off;
- allowing disability leave.

Promotion

When employees are candidates for promotion, disabled employees should not be discriminated against because of their disability, perceived disability, association with someone with a disability or something linked to their disability.

For example, an employer should not assume, without asking the employee, that they would find the more senior role too stressful because of their disability.

Training

Withholding training from an employee because of their disability, perceived disability, association with someone with a disability, or something linked to their disability, would be discriminatory.

An employer must make reasonable adjustments to training, and should not assume that the employee cannot benefit from training.

A person with a learning disability may learn differently to a person without that disability, and may need extra time to absorb information or be allowed to absorb information in a different way. For example, a disabled person might learn more easily if they watch how to do the job rather than be expected to learn through written instructions.

Dismissal

Before arriving at a decision to dismiss a disabled employee for incapacity (they are not reasonably capable of doing their job) and to justify the dismissal an employer is likely to have to show the following:

- they followed a fair capability procedure before arriving at the decision to dismiss;
- they have made all reasonable adjustments;
- the disabled employee is not capable of doing the job even with required adjustments;
- there is no alternative employment which would be suitable for the disabled employee.

If the disabled employee has been absent from work for an extended period because of the disability, before arriving at a decision to dismiss, it is likely that the employer will need to:

- show that the extended absence is causing difficulties to the business;
- obtain a medical report (subject to the *Access to Medical Reports Act 1988*) and a prognosis as to whether the employee will be able to return to work within a reasonable time-frame;
- obtain a medical opinion as to whether the employee will be able to do their job to a reasonable standard when they return to work.
- obtain a medical opinion on the question of possible further adjustments.

When giving judgment on a claim of disability discrimination, an employment tribunal may take into consideration an employer's resources and its size, and the adverse impact the long-term absence of the employee had on the business, but the onus will be on the employer to show the adverse impact.

Unless an employer has considered and made all possible reasonable adjustments a dismissal is likely to be both unfair and discriminatory.

Redundancy

When an employer needs to make some staff redundant there is a risk that a disabled employee who is chosen for redundancy will allege disability discrimination.

To minimise the risk of a disability discrimination claim an employer must ensure that a disabled employee was not disadvantaged in any way in the selection procedure, either in the selection criteria used or in the overall way the redundancy procedure was managed.

In particular, in most cases, an employer should avoid using *absence from work* as one of the criteria in the selection procedure when disabled employees are in the *pool* of candidates for redundancy and have taken significant time off work because of their disability.

However, what is reasonable will always depend on all the circumstances of an individual case.

Other Bullet Point Booklets

Disciplinary Procedures
National Minimum Wage
Employment Contracts
Defending Employment Tribunal Claims
TUPE
Staff Handbooks
Settlement Agreements
Redundancy
Recruitment
Sick Pay
Maternity
Homeworking

Bullet Point Booklets are available from Amazon as ebooks and in print.

About Worklaw

Worklaw specialises in giving help and advice and training to employers on all aspects of UK employment law.

Worklaw is comprised of a group of self-employed independent employment law consultants and human resource managers who all work from home. This means that *Worklaw* can charge much less than its competitors for the same level of service to clients as we do not have office overheads and expensive support staff.

Since 2002, *Worklaw* consultants have represented employers in every employment tribunal in England and Wales and in the Employment Appeal Tribunal, plus employment tribunals in Edinburgh and Glasgow. *Worklaw* also provides other employment law services, including;

- human resource management on long or short retainers;
- employment law training and seminars;
- employment tribunal representation for a fixed fee;
- drafting employment contracts, staff handbooks, etc.

email: robin@worklaw.co.uk
or visit Worklaw's website:
https://www.worklaw.co.uk

- LaTeX typesetting
- and cover design
- by Quaystone Books
- www.thrillers.pub

Printed in Great Britain
by Amazon

45726502R00020